Selah

STUDYING GOD'S SONGBOOK

Betty Henderson

journeyforth®

Greenville, South Carolina

Selah—Studying God's Songbook
Betty Henderson

Design by Craig Oesterling
Page layout by Michael Boone

© 2014 by BJU Press
Greenville, South Carolina 29614
JourneyForth Books is a division of BJU Press

Printed in the United States of America
All rights reserved

ISBN 978-1-60682-854-0
eISBN 978-1-60682-856-4

15   14   13   12   11   10   9   8   7   6   5   4   3   2   1

This study of Psalms is lovingly dedicated to the members of the choir at Colonial Hills Baptist Church, Indianapolis, Indiana. For more than twenty years, it has been my special blessing to sing "in the ways of the Lord" (Psalm 138:5) with this group of devoted servants.

Until we sing together in Emmanuel's Land, may we always be found joyfully serving and singing the praise and glory of His lovely Name!

"And he hath put a new song in my mouth, even praise unto our God."
—Psalm 40:3

Contents

This Way to Happiness!

For the Lord knoweth the way of the righteous.
—Psalm 1:6

Scripture to read: Psalm 1:1–6

The great book of Psalms begins with a little song of only six verses. It has been called a faithful gateway to the entire beloved book, and it is rightly called the Psalm of the Two Ways. The human author of Psalm 1 is not known, but its foundational theme is one that is often found in God's Word: the life of the righteous person contrasted with the life of the ungodly.

This important psalm is short and to the point, full of timely counsel for all who seek after true happiness. Through this psalm, the Holy Spirit tells all men and women where to find happiness. A happy life is always marked by right character that leads to right choices. Throughout Scripture God has placed warnings about broad paths and narrow ones, light and darkness, and life and death. Psalm 1 is another place where He warns us that not all lifestyles please Him, and some definitely lead to sorrow and death.

Psalm 1 is a very old song, but like all of God's Word it is very up to date. Throughout the centuries, God has observed the hearts of all people. He has not looked at their skin color, nationality, position in society, or ability. He knows well our heart condition and that of every person who has ever lived. He knows all who have chosen righteousness as well as those who have chosen paths of unrighteousness. Oh, what a difference our choices make!

The Conduct and Character of a Righteous Man (Ps. 1:1–3)

1. What is the first word of this first psalm? What does *blessed* mean?

   _____

   Where do people often look for happiness?

   _____

   _____

2. Psalm 1:1 states three negative behaviors believers are to avoid if they would honor God. What is the first one?

   _____

   Walking, or having occasional, casual contact with those who have no fear of God is dangerous for believers. Why is this true? The following verses will help you with your answer.

   Proverbs 4:14–17

   _____

   _____

   Proverbs 19:27–28

   _____

   _____

1 Corinthians 15:33

_____

_____

3. What is the second warning given to believers in 1:1?

    _____

    Does this statement mean we're never to befriend sinners? Why or why not?

    _____

    _____

4. We have noted the progression that comes when we first walk with the ungodly and then begin standing in the way with them. According to 1:1, what is the final step downward?

    _____

    Adopting the scornful, hypocritical attitude of the ungodly can lead to a seared conscience.

    > At last he feels a comparative rest from uneasiness of conscience and doubts of mind that once frequently disturbed him, and he begins to scoff like his friends, reviling good men, and mocking at things sacred. Thus he sits in "the seat of the scornful."[1]

5. How might the following present-day technologies cause believers to sit in the presence of scorners?

    Television:

    _____

    Movies:

    _____

Radio:

_____

Websites:

_____

Social media:

_____

6. A godly woman will choose her best friends carefully. How can spending too much time in the company of those who reject God weaken her?

_____

> Ungodly people are all around us. . . . The ungodly can live in our homes, work with us, be among our best friends. Taking their advice is fatal. The blessed person does not slow down to walk with them. If he does, his walk will soon come to an immobilizing standstill.[2]

The little word *but* begins the second verse of this timely psalm. It is a signal that a change of thought is approaching. We have been considering the things a righteous person doesn't do. Now the psalmist is ready to point us to the delight of soaking our souls in the Word of God.

7. According to 1:2, a godly woman desires to have more than a casual acquaintance with the Bible. She considers her time with God to be a delightful part of her day. What does it mean to delight ourselves in the law of the Lord?

_____

8. David was a man who took great delight in the Scripture available to him (the first five books of the Bible). Read the following verses and note how he described his love for the Word.

Psalm 119:24

_____

Psalm 119:92

_____

Psalm 119:143

_____

Psalm 119:174

_____

> Perhaps . . . you do not walk in the way of the un-
> godly (verse 1), but let me ask you—is your delight
> in the law of God? Do you study God's Word? Do
> you make it . . . your best companion and hourly
> guide? If not, [the blessings of verse 3] belong not
> to you.[3]

In the first two verses of this great psalm, the author has revealed requirements every believer must meet if she would have
the blessing of God on her life. In 1:3 we are now given some of
the wonderful rewards that come from delighting ourselves in
God and His Word.

9. After reading 1:3, write down the four phrases that
   describe the life of the righteous.

   _____

   _____

10. Why do you think God used trees to symbolize the
    righteous?

    _____

    _____

There are many kinds of "trees" in God's family forest:
tiny seedlings, strong shade trees, evergreens, weeping

willows, giant redwoods, fruitful trees, barren and
diseased trees, and some that are withered.

Why do some trees—or believers—grow taller and
stronger than others?

_____

_____

Why do some produce much fruit, while others produce
little?

_____

_____

Why do some eventually wither and dry up spiritually?

_____

_____

11. The most important part of a tree is its roots. There will
be no fruit without a strong, well-watered, and well-fed
root system. List some things a godly woman can do, with
God's help, to keep her spiritual roots fed and well
watered.

_____

_____

What is the present condition of your spiritual roots?
Are they healthy, well-watered, and well-fed, or parched
and almost withered? What will you do to improve your
"root system"?

_____

_____

A church or Christian ministry composed of believers
with weak and shallow roots will be a weak organization
and will produce little fruit for the Master. Is your

spiritual condition helping or hindering your church or ministry?

The Conduct and Character of the Unrighteous Person (Ps. 1: 4–6)

The second section of this instructive psalm describes the person who is the opposite of the righteous man who is firmly planted, fruitful, and prosperous in his life.

12. In contrast to the towering, well-watered tree described earlier, what one word does the Holy Spirit use in 1:4 to describe the person who chooses to live without God?

---

13. In what way is chaff a picture of instability and uselessness?

> Chaff refers to the dry fragments of the shell-type coverings of grain seeds. After the coverings are broken off, the light chaff and the heavy seeds are separated by tossing them into the air so that the wind blows away the worthless chaff.[4]

14. How are the ungodly further described in the following verses? What is their greatest sin?

Psalm 10:4

Psalm 36:1–4

Proverbs 1:28–33

_____

_____

Why are the ungodly lost? Because they will not submit to Christ and His Word. They prefer the counsel of the ungodly to the "whole counsel of God" (Acts 20:27).[5]

15. According to Psalm 1:5, the unrighteous man or woman will not stand guiltless at the last judgment. Read Revelation 20:11–15, and describe such a person as he or she stands before the omniscient Creator.

    _____

    _____

    According to Revelation 20:15, what determines one's final eternal destiny?

    _____

    _____

16. Each of us was born into unrighteousness (wickedness). How, then, can we become righteous? See Romans 3:21–24, Ephesians 2:8–9, and Titus 3:4–7 for help with your answer.

    _____

    _____

    _____

17. What was the date, or occasion, when you became righteous through faith in Jesus Christ and your name was written in God's Book of Life?

    _____

    _____

How was the news of your salvation received in heaven?
See Luke 15:10.

_____

_____

18. What loving invitation does God freely offer to the
wicked in Isaiah 55:7?

_____

_____

Why, then, do the ungodly perish?

_____

_____

"The Lord is . . . not willing that any should perish, but
that all should come to repentance." (2 Peter 3:9)

19. The final verse in Psalm 1 is yet another wonderful
promise for those who are righteous. What is this
promise?

_____

_____

What solemn final thought is also given here about the
ungodly?

_____

_____

Oh! to be without a Savior,
With no hope nor refuge nigh;
Can it be, O blessed Savior,
One without Thee dares to die?[6]

Frank M. Davis

Selah—Pause and Think on These Things

- Each of us fits into one of the two categories mentioned by the writer of this psalm. Are you a happy, productive believer today, or are you living a hopeless life without Christ? There are only two paths for us to walk on, and each person chooses the path of his life. Oh, what a difference our choices will make for all of eternity!

- Believer, how firmly planted is your tree? Are your roots and leaves healthy or withered? How much fruit are you bearing for the Master? Under the power of God's Spirit, believers must continue producing fruit until the Lord calls them home. See Psalm 92:12–14.

- Earlier in the lesson we spoke of the varied kinds of trees in "God's eternal forest." Who are the great believers—evergreens and redwoods—that have encouraged you spiritually? Who are the young trees and tiny seedlings and weeping willows that you can encourage?

- God is not willing that the ungodly should perish. The blood of Jesus Christ His Son cleanses (people) from *all* sin (1 John 1:7). Are we crying out daily for the salvation of those walking in darkness toward an eternity without Christ?

> O how vast the blessings to the man who flees
> Company with those who love iniquity!
> But in God's instruction he takes deep delight,
> Fixing his attention on it day and night.
>
> As a tree well-watered cannot be removed,
> So the righteous prosper, ever yielding fruit.
> But ungodly sinners like the chaff will be:
> Windblown throughout life, then lost eternally.
>
> Lovers of the Lord's Law are supremely blessed:
> Rooted firm and fruitful, strong through every test.[7]

Joseph Tyrpak

Songs for Waking
or Sleeping

I laid me down and slept; I awaked;
for the Lord sustained me.
—Psalm 3:5

Scripture to read: Psalms 3 and 4

As we open the door of these two comforting psalms, we notice David authored both. They were probably written while he was on the run from his rebellious son Absalom. Forced to flee his royal palace, David and a few of his faithful followers sought to hide themselves from the anger and danger of countless enemies. (See 2 Sam. 15:1–37.)

Psalm 3 is known as a morning psalm and opens with David laying his troubles before his God. From the wilderness he cried unto the one who was his shield and salvation. His confidence in the Almighty allowed him to lie on the cold, hard ground and go sound asleep. Morning came, and he arose knowing that God would rise up as his Defender.

Psalm 4, the evening psalm, also opens with David crying out to God for help. Weeks had passed, and Israel's king was still fleeing from place to place. In his loneliness and grief, he continually sought God's presence and comfort. He testified freely to the gladness placed in his heart by his God, and then he ended the psalm as he fell asleep, surrounded by heavenly safety.

The little word *selah* was purposely used by the author five times in these sixteen verses. Some think the word means to stop, be silent, and consider carefully the words just read. Others believe *selah* refers to a musical pause, the precise definition being unknown. I prefer the first meaning, believing the word calls us to faithful observation and meditation. The two great psalms before us deserve much of both.

Psalm 3—The Morning Psalm

David's Trouble (Ps. 3:1–2)

1. In the first two verses, how did David describe the many miseries that surrounded him?

   _____

   _____

2. What wicked statement did David's enemies make against his God (3:2)?

   _____

   _____

   Note that David ended 3:2 with the word *selah*. Why do you think he instructed us to stop and consider carefully the words we just read?

   _____

   _____

3. If someone said that your situation was hopeless and that your God would not help or deliver you, how would you answer them?

   _____

   _____

The apostle Paul was another servant of God who often faced great trials. What inspiring words of hope did he write for all believers in Romans 8:35–39?

_____

_____

David's Trust (Ps. 3:3–4)

4. Read 3:3. What words of confidence did David give in answer to his slanderous foes?

_____

_____

How is God a shield for all of His people?

_____

_____

5. We praise God that He was the "lifter up" of David's head (3:3). When is the last time He lifted up your head from the pit of discouragement or distress?

_____

_____

Do you know someone who needs to be reminded that God is still the "lifter up" of drooping heads? How will you share this verse of hope with them?

_____

_____

> Though I hang my head in sorrow, [He] shall very soon lift it up in joy and thanksgiving. What a divine trio of mercies is contained in this verse: defense for the defenseless, glory for the despised, and joy for the comfortless.[1]

6. On the run from those who would silence him, David used his voice for what important purpose (3:4)?

_____

Read the last part of 3:4. What was he very confident about?

_____

David's many enemies were lifting up their voices in slander against him and his God. God had lifted up his head with encouragement, and now David lifted up his voice to God. He had no doubt that he would be heard and helped by the one who was his shield and his glory. Selah!

David's Testimony (Ps. 3:5–8)

7. What testimonies of God's goodness did David give in 3:5?

_____

Is it still possible for God's children to lie down and sleep soundly even when surrounded by great storms? Why or why not?

_____

_____

The book of Psalms contains countless promises from our great God. I like to call these promises "soft pillows" where I can lay my head and heart and go soundly to sleep. Some of the "soft pillows" I have used many times include Psalm 23:1–6; 27:13–14; 34:17–19; and 138:7–8. What "soft pillows" of promise have you recently rested on?

_____

_____

8. After a good night's sleep in his wilderness suite, what new confidence in God did David express (3:6)?

_____

_____

What request did he make of God in 3:7?

_____

This request was followed by a testimony of God's past actions on his behalf. How had God made David's enemies useless?

_____

_____

9. Read 3:8. David closed his morning psalm with two important truths. What are they?

_____

_____

Do you believe that salvation comes only from God? What Bible verses show that salvation does not come from man's good works or from any church, but through faith in the Son of God alone?

_____

_____

A man on the run, hiding from a wicked, rebellious son, still believed that God blesses and cares for His own. "Thy blessing is upon thy people. Selah." Wonderful words that we need to stop and meditate on, whether we're surrounded by times of joy or the pain of our own wilderness.

Psalm 4—The Evening Psalm

The circumstances of this psalm are similar to those of Psalm 3. David continued on the run from Absalom and his armies, but those many days in the wilderness also found him running continually to God. In this short psalm, David spoke first to God, and then he had timely words for those who had become his enemies. The final three verses of this brief psalm contain a request and a testimony. David then pillowed his head on the person and promises of God and safely slept.

Words for God (Ps. 4:1)

10. As he began his evening song, what name did David use to address his God?

> *God of my righteousness* deserves notice, since it is not used in any other part of Scripture. It means, Thou art the author, the witness, the maintainer, the judge, and the rewarder of my righteousness; to Thee I appeal from the harsh judgments of men.[2]

11. According to 4:1, what divine assistance had David previously received?

What two requests did he now bring to God?

Words for the Ungodly (Ps. 4:2–5)

12. Read 4:2. What questions did the king have for those who were seeking to dethrone him? (Use a study Bible or a dictionary to define *vanity* and *leasing*.)

Why do you think David inserted the word *selah* after he had described the sins of his enemies?

_____

_____

13. According to 4:3–4, what specific truths did David want the ungodly to remember?

_____

_____

What does being "set apart" for God mean, and who are the people that God sets apart to do His work?

_____

_____

14. What New Testament instructions did Paul and John give to those who would be set apart to serve God? See Romans 12:1–3, 2 Corinthians 6:14, and 1 John 2:15–16 for help with your answer.

_____

_____

Words for God (Ps. 4:6–8)

15. After making a statement in 4:6 about many who were faithless, what did the king ask his God to do?

_____

_____

What similar requests did he make in the following verses?

Psalm 31:16

_____

Psalm 69:17

Psalm 119:135

As Israel's king reigning in Jerusalem, David was accustomed to people from far and near seeking favored opportunities to be in his royal presence. But it wasn't the pomp and ceremony of royalty that David craved. No! He could not bear to be without the daily presence and favor of his King. And so may it be with us. Scottish hymn writer Elizabeth Clephane expressed the same desire when she wrote these lovely words: "I ask no other sunshine than the sunshine of His face."[3]

16. The thought of God smiling upon him there in the wilderness caused great gladness in David's heart (4:7). We note in 4:8 that he didn't sit up to watch and worry about his many enemies. According to the verse, what did he do?

In this same verse, what final statement of confidence did he make about his God?

Selah—Pause and Think on These Things

- David was undoubtedly thankful for God's day care and His night care as he sought wilderness hiding places from his enemies. That same day care and night care is still available to God's children who are living centuries after His servant David.

The key that opens the door to such care is found in Joshua 1:8

and Psalm 1:2—meditating in the word of God.

- At the close of your day, do you lie down in peace and go to sleep? Remembering and meditating on the truths of Psalms 3 and 4 will bring rest to your soul and sleep for your body. David's God is ours also, and "He that keepeth [us] will not slumber. Behold, he that keepeth Israel shall neither slumber nor sleep" (Ps. 121:3–4).

- In the midst of David's many troubles, God lifted up his weary head. Perhaps your own head is presently weighed down with grief or trouble. Isn't our God still able to lift up the heads and hearts of His beloved people? Cry unto the Lord because He will not fail to hear and help you.

- Set-apart servants are still needed in present-day churches and ministries. To be set apart means every area of our lives are sur- rendered to do His will. One of my favorite set-apart servants from the past is hymn writer Frances Havergal. Since Victorian times, her hymn of consecration has been used to help God's people understand all it means to be a set-apart servant.

> Take my life and let it be
> Consecrated, Lord, to Thee;
> Take my moments and my days,
> Let them flow in ceaseless praise,
> Let them flow in ceaseless praise.
>
> Take my hands and let them move
> At the impulse of Thy love;
> Take my feet and let them be
> Swift and beautiful for Thee,
> Swift and beautiful for Thee.
>
> Take my love—my God, I pour
> At Thy feet its treasure-store;
> Take myself, and I will be
> Ever, only, all for Thee,
> Ever, only, all for Thee.[4]

Frances Havergal

When I Consider

*When I consider thy heavens, the work of thy
fingers, the moon and the stars,
which thou hast ordained;
what is man that thou art mindful of Him?*
—Psalm 8:3–4

Scripture to read: Psalm 8:1–9

Psalm 8 is an exquisite little song of praise. As we read its
nine verses, we note that its author, David, made no requests of
God. (There are only a handful of Psalms about which this can
be said; among them are Psalms 103, 104, and 145.) Instead of
seeking help from God, David sought to show us the greatness,
power, and majesty that belong to God alone.

As we enter the front door of the psalm, we read the author's
words as he declares the magnificence of God's name. We are
then led to consider His creation and His love and care for sinful
people. After reading one of the greatest questions in the Bible,
we exit out the back door of Psalm 8 singing hallelujahs to our
wonderful God!

The psalms are often referred to in the New Testament, and
Jesus quoted from Psalm 8 at least once. The Holy Spirit directed

Paul to include words from this little psalm in 1 Corinthians 15, and the writer of Hebrews also referred to it in the second chapter of his great book. From this holy repetition we are reminded of the psalm's importance to God's people.

Let us now open the front door of Psalm 8 that we may learn new reasons to praise and adore our loving God!

Considering His Name (Ps. 8:1)

1. In 8:1, what exclamation of greatness did David make in regarding the name of our Lord?

   _____

   _____

2. Sadly, God's majestic and glorious name has never been revered in all the earth. How do sinful people most often use His holy name?

   _____

   _____

3. After reading the following Scriptures, please note how each writer described God's name.

   Nehemiah 9:5

   _____

   Psalm 99:3

   _____

   Psalm 113:1–3

   _____

   Matthew 6:9

   _____

4. In the following verses, how are we commanded to respond to His great name?

Psalm 69:3

Psalm 96:8

Psalm 115:1

---

5. According to Philippians 2:9–11, how will people of all centuries eventually respond to the mighty name of God's Son?

> Lord, our Lord, Thy glorious name,
> All Thy wondrous works proclaim.
>
> In the heavens with radiant signs
> Evermore Thy glory shines.[1]
>
> *The Psalter*

Considering His Enemies (Ps. 8:2)

Psalm 8:1 helps our hearts to focus on the greatness and glory of the one who is God alone. It is fitting that the mouths of adults, as well as mouths of little children, should proclaim His majesty. In verse 2 of this brief psalm, David reminded us, however, that not all people praise God. Some do not believe He is Creator of all things, and in their pride and rebellion, they declare Him to be their enemy!

6. What are the sources of sinful man's hatred of God? Read Psalm 10:4 and Jeremiah 17:9 to find an answer.

---

7. Infidels refuse to praise Him, but according to 8:2, what weak and helpless creatures has God often used to quiet His enemies?

> Infant lips Thou dost ordain
> Wrath and vengeance to restrain
> Weakest means fulfill Thy will,
> Mighty enemies to still.[2]
>
> *The Psalter*

8. Turn to Matthew 21:15–16. Whose voices were used to to praise Christ in the Jerusalem temple? How did the enemies of the Savior respond to their words of praise to the "Son of David?" How did Jesus respond?

> He who delights in the songs of angels is pleased to honor Himself in the eyes of His enemies by the praises of little children. What a contrast between the glory above the heavens (vs. 1), and the mouths of babes and |unweaned children|! Yet by both the name of God is made excellent.[3]

Considering His Creation (Ps. 8:3–8)

The psalmist now turned from the praise of infants and the quieting of infidels to think about the awesome work of God's hands and fingers.

9. Read 8:3. What three magnificent works of creation did David first muse upon?

As a shepherd, and later as a man hiding from King Saul and others, David had spent countless nights surrounded by the glories of God's heaven. Night after night he took time to view and consider not only the greatness of creation, but also the power and might of the Creator! When is the last time you spent time observing and considering the heavenly bodies that continuously declare the glory of God? How they show us what insignificant beings we truly are!

> The moon is about 2,160 miles across and 238,857 miles away from the earth. . . . We are about 24 trillion miles from the nearest star. The North Star is 90 times that distance away. There are billions of stars in our galaxy. The scale of the solar system and the galaxy staggers the mind![4]

10. God's brilliant display in the heavens astounded David. But according to 8:4, what amazed him even more?

Read Psalm 144:3. What similar thought did David present in this verse?

11. It is a mystery that the almighty, all-knowing God of heaven stooped to ask for our love and our fellowship. According to 1 John 3:1, what has He lavished upon all who will receive His salvation?

12. We know from Genesis 1 that God created man. David affirmed this truth in 8:5. In this verse, how did David describe God's great kindness and honor to sinful man?

"A little lower than the angels" is God's estimate of the human race. We are not "a little higher than the beasts." Charles Darwin described man as "the most efficient animal ever to emerge on earth." What a degrading view of man! Man was made by an act of God, and made in the image and likeness of God.[5]

13. Read 8:6–8. What authority did God entrust to humans?

What specific creatures did David list as being under the rule of man?

Read the following statement by Victorian preacher Charles Spurgeon. Although written almost 140 years ago, his words are very up-to-date!

Let none of us permit the possession of any earthly creature to be a snare to us, but let us remember that we are to reign over them, and not allow them to reign over us.[6]

14. Read Romans 1:25. Instead of worshiping our divine Creator, what do wicked people often choose to worship?

How do twenty-first-century people sometimes allow earthly creatures to become a snare to them?

15. David concluded his song as he began it. In 8:9, what is his closing doxology to his majestic God?

_____

_____

Selah—Pause and Think on These Things

- Our Lord, whose name is great and glorious, knows our names! He also is fully acquainted with all of our ways (Ps. 139:3) and yet loves us with an everlasting love (Jer. 31:3). The King of Heaven has stooped to ask of us the love of our poor hearts. O Lord, our Lord, we bless Your holy name forever!

- Our Lord, whose hands fashioned the heavens and the moon and stars, promises to hold our hands in our hours of greatest joy and greatest grief (Isa. 41:13). When we are weak, He holds us up with His right hand of righteousness (Isa. 41:10). O Lord, our Lord, we bless Your mighty name forever!

- Our Lord is ever mindful of us. He made us, and He knows our frame. He remembers that we are dust (Ps. 103:14). He is our Father, and He has pity for all who are so pitiful (Ps. 103:13). O Lord, our Lord, we bless Your lovely name forever!

When I consider the work of Thy hands,
The sun, moon and stars above,
What is man that Thou thinkest of him
Who is so unworthy of Thy love?

O Lord, our Lord, how majestic is Thy name.
Mountains, valleys, all creation tells Thy fame.
Heavens declare it, all Thy wondrous works proclaim;
O Lord, our Lord, how majestic is Thy name.[7]

Ron Hamilton

Declare His Glory!

The heavens declare the glory of God;
and the firmament sheweth his handiwork.
—Psalm 19:1

Scripture to Read: Psalm 19:1–14

There are numerous reasons why David is called the "sweet psalmist of Israel" (2 Sam. 23:1). Perhaps the great psalm before us is just one of those reasons since it is surely one of his sweetest and most-loved songs.

David begins Psalm 19 by turning our eyes upward to behold the vigilant, nonverbal preachers of the sky. Since time began, the stars and all the lights of heaven have testified that "the hand which made us is divine." Almost immediately he then directs our eyes to see another of God's great wonders: the Scriptures. In just three verses, we are given various names or titles for the Word, a brief description of its worth, and the effect it can have on each heart that reads it.

Last of all, he directs our eyes inward, as he cries out to God for help in dealing with the sins that so frequently plagued his soul. King David was well acquainted with his sinful self. Are we also acquainted with our own secret and presumptuous sins?

In the final verse of Psalm 19, we will find the psalmist looking to his Rock and his Redeemer. He prayed for acceptable words and thoughts that would enable him to declare God's glory to those around him. How we praise God for another of David's great hymns of praise to God!

The Skies Declare His Glory (Ps. 19:1–6)

1. According to 19:1, what do the heavens and the firmament specifically declare about God? What does this mean?

   _____

   _____

2. Verse 2 reveals that these "celestial missionaries" work around the clock, never growing weary of their divine work. What are they doing day after day?

   _____

   What is their responsibility night after night?

   _____

3. Read 19:3–4. How extensive is their area of witness?

   _____

   The greatness of creation points to a mighty Creator. According to Romans 1:19–23, what has been the response of men to the universal message of our great Creator?

   _____

   Despite this universal message that pours out day and night to the entire world, most people ignore it and reject God because they want to live as they please. The repeated question "Are people lost who have never heard about Jesus?" has two answers: (1) Yes, they are lost because God speaks to them all

day long, and they refuse to listen; (2) What are you
doing about getting the message to these people?[1]

Before moving on to the second faithful way God reveals
Himself to man, we need to consider David's special reference
to the marvel that is the sun (19:4–6).

4. God made the sun as a greater light to rule the day (Gen.
   1:16). What would happen to us and our world if the sun
   didn't shine?

   _____

5. What word picture did David paint in 19:4–6 to help
   us understand the daily cycle of the sun? (Note that the
   word *tabernacle*, as used here, means a tent or dwelling.)

   _____

   _____

6. Read 2 Peter 3:10–13. What promise did Peter give
   regarding the end of the heavens and the destruction of
   the earth?

   _____

   What additional promise is also given in 19:13?

   _____

7. According to Revelation 21:27, who will dwell in this
   new heaven and new earth?

   _____

   Why does the new heaven have no need of the sun or
   moon? Read Revelation 21:23 and 22:5

   _____

   Fair is the sunshine
   Fairer still the moonlight,
   And all the twinkling starry host;
   Jesus shines brighter,

Jesus shines purer
Than all the angels
Heaven can boast![2]

Author unknown

The Scriptures Declare His Glory (Ps. 19:7–11)

The heavens and the sun tell us of God's power, might, and greatness. But if we would know of His love, grace, mercy, and redemption, then we must look into the Scriptures and not up into the sky. David stood in awe of God's wonders in the world, but we see in 19: 7–11 that he loved and valued God's wonders in the Word most of all.

8. Six names, or titles, are given for God's Word in 19:7–9. What are they?

L_____ of the Lord
T_____ of the Lord
S_____ of the Lord
C_____ of the Lord
F_____ of the Lord
J_____ of the Lord

9. In these same verses, six adjectives are used to describe God's Word. List these below.

P_____ P_____

S_____ C_____

R_____ T_____

Who is the Author of the Bible? How do we know God's Word is perfect, pure, true, and so forth? See 2 Timothy 3:16 and 2 Peter 1:20–21 for your answer.

10. We also find in verses 19:7–9 the divine effects, or ministries, Scripture has on the hearts of those who seek to know and to obey it. What are these?

C _____ the soul   E _____ the eyes

M _____ the simple   E _____ forever

R _____ the heart   R _____ altogether

How did God use His Word to convert your soul?

_____

_____

How has the Word brought rejoicing to your life?

_____

_____

What wisdom, and joy, have you recently received from the Word?

_____

_____

11. David isn't finished with the glories of God's Word! In 19:10–11, he tells us of the profit and pleasure that come with the knowledge of this holy book. What are these?

_____

_____

His Servants Declare His Glory (Ps. 19:13–14)

Before writing the lovely closing prayer of this great psalm, the Holy Spirit led David to pen words of warning and counsel for believers who desire to declare the glory of God. From experience he knew well the destructive effects of sin in a believer's life. Through the Scriptures comes the knowledge of sin, and the psalmist marveled at the extent and awfulness of that sin. May David's sensitivity toward sin also be present in our lives.

12. Read 19:12–13 and answer these questions:

What is the meaning of the words *secret faults*?

_____

What is the meaning of *presumptuous sins*?

_____

13. According to 19:13, what fear did David express about secret and presumptuous sins?

_____

_____

14. Is there any sin that presently has rule, or dominion, over you? Explain.

_____

_____

15. The final verse of Psalm 19 is one of the loveliest found in the heavenly songbook. What appeal did David make to God regarding his words and thoughts?

_____

_____

What do you think the word *acceptable* means?

_____

16 In Romans 12:1, what similar truth about living acceptably did Paul stress in his instructions to believers?

_____

_____

Selah—Pause and Think on These Things.

Unless we have a personal relationship with the Lord so that God is our Father and Jesus is our Redeemer, what we see in creation and what we read in the Bible will not do us much good. The Word in the hand is fine, the Word in the head is better, but the Word in the heart is what transforms us and matures us in Christ.[3]

- May our desire as redeemed ones always be to have our hearts, our thoughts, and our service acceptable to our great Redeemer. I believe David and Paul offered themselves on their private altars of sacrifice everyday. They climbed up on the altar and acknowledged to God their desire to declare His glory. Is our all on the altar of sacrifice laid? How are we declaring His glory?

- Surely God's world is "full of [His] riches" (Ps. 104:24). We have learned from Psalm 19 that His Word is also full of great riches (Ps. 19:10). How we praise Him for the wonders of His world, but we especially give thanks for the wonders of His Word!

The Lord's law is complete;
It makes the soul arise:
The Lord's decree is sure;
It makes the simple wise:
The statutes of the Lord are right,
Imparting to the heart delight!

The Lord's command is pure;
Light on the eyes it pours:
The Lord's fear is unstained;
Forever it endures:
The judgments of the Lord are true,
And altogether righteous, too![4]

Scottish Psalter

"What Am I to Do?"

Lead me in thy truth, and teach me:
for thou art the God of my salvation;
on thee do I wait all the day.
—Psalm 25:5

Scripture to read: Psalm 25:1–22

In this lesson we are glad to dig deeper into yet another in-spiring psalm from David's pen. It apparently was written on the occasion of serious, but unrevealed, trouble in his life. Like many of us, David had plenty of troubles to deal with, and be-lievers of all centuries are grateful that the Holy Spirit directed him to record his thoughts and burdens. Psalm 25 presents to us truths that will help us handle our own times of sorrows and distress biblically.

In Lesson Three, we noted that when writing Psalm 8, David's pen flowed with only praise to his mighty God. No prayer re-quests or cries for help were found. Not so in Psalm 25, where over fifteen requests are recorded. We will especially notice his numerous cries for heavenly guidance: "Show me." "Teach me." "Lead me." Through these words David is saying, "What am I to do, Lord?" Thankfully the answer to this question is woven throughout Psalm 25. He was to pray, he was to fear the Lord, and he was to trust God. Good counsel not only for David, but also for all who love David's God!

I Am to Pray (Ps. 25:1–7)

1. After lifting up his soul to Jehovah God in verse 1, what brief statement of faith follows in 25:2?

   _____

   What two requests did he also make in 25:2?

   _____

   _____

   > The Hebrew word used for our word *ashamed* refers to the shame "that comes from failure, either a personal failure or the failure of something or someone that has been trusted."[1]

2. In light of the above definition, write your own paraphrase of 25:3.

   _____

   _____

   According to David, who will not be brought to shame? Who did he say would certainly be brought to shame?

   _____

   _____

3. David abhorred the thought of being a treacherous, shameful person like those he described in 25:2–3. Therefore, what help did he seek from God in verses 25:4–5?

   _____

   _____

4. What things did he want God to show him and teach him?

_____

How did he ask God to lead him?

_____

5. Read the last part of 25:5 again. What statement did the psalmist make about waiting on God?

_____

What does it means to wait on God? Use Scripture to help with your answer.

_____

_____

6. What are you presently waiting upon God to do in your life?

_____

What Bible promises are you claiming as you wait? List some of them below.

_____

_____

I will not take one step until I know
Which way it is that You would have me go![2]

7. The final request of David's first prayer in Psalm 25 is found in 25:6–7. Here we note one word that is used three times. What is it?

_____

What two things did he want God to remember?

_____

What did he want God to forget?

_____

8. How did David describe God in 25:6–7?

_____

_____

What one word did he use to describe the mercies of God? Why should we be grateful for this compassionate word?

_____

_____

9. We have all been blessed by the *tender mercies* God has so freely bestowed on us. David often wrote of his longing for such mercies in his life. How did he speak of God's *tender mercies* in the verses below?

Psalm 51:1

_____

Psalm 103:4

_____

Psalm 119:156

_____

Psalm 145:9

_____

> Was there ever a sweeter sound than this—"tender mercies"? He who has been grievously afflicted . . . is the only person who knows the meaning of such choice language.[3]

I Am to Fear the Lord (Ps. 25:8–14)

In this portion of Psalm 25, we have David's meditation on the character and work of his God. After reading 25:8–14, answer these questions.

10. In these verses, what words did he use to describe God?

_____

What are some of the works of God that David mentioned?

_____

_____

11. In 25:9, what description is given of the person that God guides and teaches?

_____

Describe someone who is *meek*.

_____

_____

12. Why does God not guide those who are proud and arrogant? For help with your answer, read these verses:

Proverbs 6:16–17

_____

Proverbs 16:5

_____

James 4:6

_____

13. According to 25:10, God gives His mercy and truth to those who walk on His paths if they _____, or obey, His covenant and His testimonies. This is a

wonderful promise from God, but it is a conditional promise that we need to carefully meditate upon.

Right in the middle of David's meditation on God is a prayer and a testimony. As he considered the goodness, tender mercy, and truth of the Lord, perhaps he was reminded how unlike God he truly was. He knew his sin caused broken fellowship with his Lord. May we be similarly sensitive about our sin.

14. What are the words of David's request in 25:11? What testimony did he give about his sin?

15. There are important instructions regarding sin in Proverbs 28:13 and 1 John 1:9. What are these?

Are there sins presently in your life that need to be confessed and forsaken?

Just and holy is Thy Name,
I am all unrighteousness;
False and full of sin I am;
Thou art full of truth and grace.[4]

Charles Wesley

16. According to 25:12–14, the blessings and the secret (or counsel) of the Lord, is especially for which people?

What do you think it means to "fear the Lord"?

Bible teachers give various opinions as to the meaning of fearing the Lord. I have always defined it as having a reverent attitude of submission and obedience to our great and merciful God for who He is, and for all He does. No man who rejects the fear of the Lord can ever find true wisdom (Prov. 1:7, 28–29).

17. According to the following verses, what blessings come to those who fear the Lord?

Psalm 34:7–9

_____

Psalm 103:11

_____

I Am to Trust (Ps. 25:15–22)

So far in this great Psalm, David has been talking to God (25:1–7) and talking about God (25:8–14). In the final verses, he wrote of keeping his eyes on God (25:15), even when surrounded by great troubles and distresses. Our hearts are touched as we read his closing prayer requests. In spite of his serious trials, he firmly declared that he was trusting in God for help and deliverance.

18. Read 25:16–21, and then describe some of the troubles the psalmist faced.

_____

_____

19. According to these verses, what kind of help was David trusting God to provide for him?

_____

_____

Selah—Pause and Think on These Things.

- We give thanks for Psalm 25 and the prayers of its human author as he sought heavenly guidance for his troubled life. At this time, David was not on the throne in Israel. However, he knew God was still on His throne, and he turned his eyes heavenward. He chose to pray, he chose to fear the Lord, and he chose to trust Him—a good pattern to follow for all who seek godly guidance.

  When we cannot see our way,
  Let us trust and still obey;
  He who bids us forward go
  Cannot fail the way to show.[5]

  Thomas Kelly

  An important principle of guidance is that God is never in a hurry. . . . This is where most of us break down: we are impatient so we act without God's guidance and then complain when things go wrong. It is Satan who says: "Hurry! Act now! It is now or never." . . . God cannot lead us if we are rushed and hurried, dashing here, there, and every-where—always responding to pressure. David was wanting, willing, and waiting to be led.[6]

- How willing are we to patiently wait "all the day"?

  Be still, my soul, thy God doth undertake,
  To guide the future, as He has the past.
  Thy hope, thy confidence, let nothing shake;
  All now mysterious shall be bright at last.
  Be still my soul, when change and tears are past,
  All safe and blessed we shall meet at last.[7]

  Katharina von Schlegel

LESSON SIX

"O Lord, I Wait on You!"

Wait on the Lord, be of good courage. . . . Wait, I say, on the Lord.
—Psalm 27:14

Scripture to read: Psalm 27:1–14

Psalm 27 is another beloved psalm from David's pen. Through it the Holy Spirit reveals David's desire to be in God's presence and his longing for heavenly help in his times of trouble. As in previous psalms, he acknowledged he had countless enemies who were seeking to devour him but could not because of the goodness of his Jehovah God.

Be sure to observe his use of personal pronouns throughout the psalm. "How delightful are the *me* and *my* of this exquisite psalm!"[1] We note also David's use of "I will" scattered throughout these fourteen verses: "I will be confident," "I will seek," "I will offer sacrifices," and "I will sing." Also, notice how certain he was of God's help when he wrote: "He shall hide me," "He shall set me on a rock," and "He shall strengthen." David had been forsaken by some family members and close friends, but he proclaimed in 27:10 that God would never leave him. Such strong confidence has brought comfort and healing to countless believers who have also been forsaken by those closest to their hearts.

Many scholars have expressed the opinion that Psalm 27 almost seems like two different psalms. As we study you will see that verses 1–6 could stand alone. This portion begins and ends with praise for the Lord. On the other hand, verses 7–14 are packed with supplications for help and guidance. The psalm ends with three firm commands and a sure word of promise.

In his lifetime, godly David spent endless days waiting on the Lord to direct and deliver him. Through the years this mighty servant also found that God was worth waiting for. Have we discovered this wonderful truth in our own lives?

David's Declarations About God (Ps. 27:1–3)

1. In 27:1, David used three familiar words to explain how important the Lord was in his life.

   Write those three words below.

   The Lord was his _____. ("trustworthy guide through life"[2])

   The Lord was his _____. (deliverer)

   The Lord was his _____. (refuge or fortress)

2. The great warrior who once fearlessly faced a giant ended the first verse with what two rhetorical questions?

   _____

   _____

   Why did he not fear the difficult events God had placed in his life? See Psalm 23:4 for help with your answer.

   _____

   _____

3. According to 27:2, what help had he received from God during times of afflictions?

_____

Past victory encouraged him to record in 27:3 what words of faith for the future?

_____

David rightly declared that the host of enemies attacking him was no match for His mighty Lord of Hosts! In Psalm 46, another of David's beloved psalms, he also announced not once, but twice, that "the Lord of hosts is with us; The God of Jacob is our refuge" (Ps. 46:7, 11). Hallelujah for our mighty Lord of Hosts, who is still the Protector of His people!

David's Devotion to God (Ps. 27:4–6)

In these three verses we are reminded why God declared that David was a man after His own heart (1 Sam. 13:14, Acts 13:22). His longing for God and the things of God was a continual passion of David's soul. Do we also "hunger and thirst after righteousness" (Matt. 5:6)?

4. What "one thing" was David constantly seeking after in his life (27:4)?

_____

How often did he wish to dwell in the house of the Lord?

_____

Why did he desire to take up residence in the Lord's house? What does this mean?

_____

We often speak of the beauty of heaven, but have we ever meditated on the beauty of our God? One author says the word *beauty*, as it is used in 27:4, means "loveliness, desirableness, all that makes God an object of affection and desire to the believer."[3]

Travelers abroad have sometimes spent time visiting very old cathedrals and churches. For centuries folks have flocked to see the beautiful architecture and stained glass windows in such places. David's desire was not to behold the beauty of the Lord's house. No! He longed to see the glorious beauty of his Lord. His hunger to draw nearer to God reminds me of these words:

> Nearer, still nearer, close to Thy heart,
> Draw me, my Savior—so precious Thou art!
> Fold me, O fold me close to Thy breast,
> Shelter me safe in that "Haven of Rest";
> Shelter me safe in that "Haven of Rest."[4]
>
> Leila Morris

5. In his "time of trouble" (27:5–6), what specific ways did the confident psalmist say God would help him?

_____

_____

In the psalms, David regularly wrote that the Lord was his rock. Like him, we too need to know the security and stability afforded us by Him who is the "rock of [our] strength" (Ps. 62:7). In the following verses, how does David describe his God?

Psalm 18:2

_____

Psalm 18:31

_____

Psalm 18:46

_____

Psalm 62:6–7

6. The first section of Psalm 27 ends with praise. In 27:6, David lifted up his soul to thank God for hiding him and helping him. What words did he use to express his joy?

David's Dependence on God (Ps. 27:7–14)

He who had stopped to sing now stopped to pray. Although far from the tabernacle of the Lord in Jerusalem, David still knew the way to his Father's throne of grace. As a good soldier, he also knew how to handle his weapons and found himself at home with his most important weapon: prayer.

7. Read 27:7–12 and list all of the prayer requests the psalmist spread before the Lord.

8. In 27:8–9, how many times did he use the phrase "thy face"?

What does it mean to "seek His face?"

> God's "face" indicates His personal presence or simply His being. Seeking His face is a primary characteristic of true believers who desire fellowship with God.[5]

When our Lord's face "shines upon us," it simply means that He is pleased with us. When His face turns from us (Ps. 143:7), it is a sign of his displeasure, and we need to search our hearts and confess our sins.

9. In 27:9, David acknowledged that God had been his helper in past days. What two requests followed this acknowledgment in 27:9–10?

How do we know that God never forsakes His children? Where do we find such promises in the Bible? (Ps. 9:10 is a good place to begin looking.)

Sadly, there are countless abandoned children in our sinful world. It is comforting to remember that our heavenly Father never forsakes His own. He has no orphan children! We should never worry that He will reject and disown us. However, we should always be concerned that we do not forsake Him. Hymnist Robert Robinson wrote that we are sometimes very "prone to leave the God [we] love."[6]

10. In 27:11, what urgent requests come from David's heart?

---

11. We read in 27:2 that David had some cruel and hateful enemies. These same enemies are referenced also in 27:12. What heavenly help did he request from the Lord in this verse?

It's obvious that David feared enemy tongues as much as enemy swords. Therefore he felt great need for the Lord's grace and guidance. It is profitable to also note that this great psalmist did not pray for an easy path, but for a plain (upright) path.

12. In 27:13, the man who slew Goliath speaks of fainting or losing hope. What kept him from such a state?

_____

Our God is all good, and He is alone good. By faith David believed His God would shower His goodness upon him. As the great soldier hunkered down in a lonely cave it surely seemed that God's goodness was nowhere to be found. Have you ever had similar thoughts? Why not stop right now and list some of the good things you have received from the Lord?

_____

_____

13. In 27:14, David ended his psalm by recording three commands and a promise. What are they?

_____

_____

14. What are some things David could have been waiting on God to accomplish in his life? (A quick review of his prayer requests in 27:7–12 may give you some clues.)

_____

_____

15. In Scripture, waiting on God suggests a confident expectation by believers that God will intervene on their behalf. What are you presently waiting to see God do in your life or the lives of those you love?

_____

What promises are you claiming as you wait?

_____

_____

Selah—Pause and Think on These Things

- I have found that most believers, when asked, will tell of their love for Psalm 27. However, when asked specifically which of the fourteen verses of the psalm are their favorites, most will declare their love for either verse 1 or verse 14. Hopefully this lesson has acquainted your heart with the great truths found in the other dozen verses! As you studied the lesson, what verses did the Holy Spirit specifically use to instruct, challenge, or encourage your heart?

- David's parting words to us in 27:14 contain the command "Wait on the Lord!" Are you a good "waiter"? What should be our attitude as we wait for God to help us? Certainly we should not wait fretfully, impatiently, or with a doubting spirit. Such waiting is that of an impatient child. As we wait, what attitudes will please God? Surely those who wait expectantly, patiently, humbly, and with confident faith will be rewarded. "I waited patiently for the Lord, and he inclined unto me; and heard my cry" (Ps. 40:1). Is this our testimony?

> We shall not grow weary of waiting upon God if we remember how long and how graciously He once waited on us.[7]

How Great Is God's Goodness!

Oh how great is thy goodness, which thou hast
laid up for them that fear thee.
—Psalm 31:19

Scripture to read: Psalm 31:1–24

The goodness of Jehovah God is a truth found throughout the book of Psalms. King David authored many of these psalms. Even as a shepherd boy he knew that God's goodness and mercy were following him daily as he walked the hills of Judea (Ps. 23:6). One of the highlights of the great psalm before us is David's enthusiastic proclamation of God's great goodness to all who walk in the fear of the Lord.

Goodness is one of God's attributes. (An attribute is something that is true about God.) When we say God is good, we are saying there is nothing but good that proceeds from Him. He shows His goodness through His love, grace, mercy, and long-suffering. He is all good, and He is alone good (Ps. 34:8; 100:5). The earth is full of His goodness (Ps. 33:5), and He is good to all (Ps. 145:9).

Psalms 30–39 have always been favorites of mine. Except for Psalm 33, all were authored by David. As you look through this group, you will find words of praise, thanksgiving, confidence, confession, forgiveness, and petition. The next five lessons in our study will find us "camping out" among this great group of heavenly hymns.

First we begin with the beautiful words of Psalm 31, which were written "to the chief Musician" in the temple. David intended the psalm to be sung in public gatherings of God's people. For our purposes in this lesson, we are dividing the psalm into four stanzas, and as we'll see, some of the words make for very sober singing! One author has called the thirty-first psalm the psalm of "misery and mercy." Saintly singers usually prefer singing of God's goodness and mercy, not stormy life events that leave us surrounded by misery. From all of David's highs and lows in the psalm before us, may we find hope and help for our own ups and downs.

He Is Good—I Will Trust (Ps. 31:1–8)

1. David's song began with a declaration of dependence on God (31:1). What is this?

    Commands to trust in Jehovah God are found throughout Scripture, and the King James Version uses the word *trust* four times in the song before us. What does it mean to put our trust in God?

2. Read 31:1–4. After declaring his faith, David proceeds to cry out to God for help. In these verses, what requests did he make?

We note in 31:2 that he desired Jehovah's full attention as he gave his urgent requests. How is this desire expressed?

_____

_____

May we remember David's words about having the very ear of God as we bring our own urgent needs to Him. How wonderful that even the weakest of saints have a listening ear that hears their pressing cries for help! His ears are always open to hear the pleadings of the righteous (Ps. 34:15)!

3. In 31:5, David moved from words about God's ears to comments about His hands. Because he faithfully trusted and communed with Jehovah, what had he willingly surrendered to his Redeemer?

_____

By the word *spirit* we may understand David to mean his life or himself. He regularly made a full commitment of his life to the protecting hand of Jehovah.

4. How often have you committed yourself fully to His care?

_____

At all times we should commit our all to Jesus' faithful hand; then, though life may hang on a thread, and adversities may multiply as the sands of the sea, our soul shall dwell at ease, and delight itself in quiet resting places.[1]

5. We find David's statement of surrender also quoted in Luke 23:46. Who spoke those words and when?

_____

6. Another of David's "trust testimonies" is found in 31:6, followed in 31:7 by words of praise and joy. According

to these two verses, there were four reasons for his gratefulness. What were these?

_____

_____

_____

_____

He Is Good—Will I Fear? (Ps. 31:9–13)

The first stanza of David's song ended on a note of rejoicing. As we begin the second stanza (31:9–13), joyful words have been replaced with a cry for mercy because of great trouble that now surrounded him. We read of his overwhelming grief and weeping eyes. The "sweet psalmist of Israel" (2 Sam. 23:1) was now sighing instead of singing.

7. Read 31:9–13. Describe the troubles and emotions that surrounded David.

_____

_____

Perhaps you can identify with David's song of woe. All of us have chapters in our lives that make for mournful singing. With the psalmist, we too sought hope and help, and such comforts seemed nowhere to be found. Let us not faint yet, for the upcoming stanza of David's song will bring new strength that produces robust singing!

> "My life is spent with grief," I cried,
> "My years consumed in groans,
> My strength decays, mine eyes are dried,
> And sorrow wastes my bones."

Slander and fear, on every side,
Seized and beset me round;
I to the throne of grace applied,
And speedy rescue found![2]

Isaac Watts

He Is Good—I Will Pray and Praise (Ps. 31:14–21)

We are glad to begin the third stanza of the song before us (31:14–21). In spite of all the king's tears and terrors, he purposes to trust and not faint. The little word *but* begins this section of the song. That little word always alerts us that a change of thought is going to take place, and what a change it is! We can put away the damp handkerchiefs used in stanza two. The verses before us are full of blessing and victory!

8. The fear of 31:13 turned into faith in verse 14. What new testimony of trust is found here?

---

9. In 31:5, David had put his soul into God's hand. In 31:15, he claims something else is also securely in those hands. What is this?

What might the words *my times* include?

These remarkable words can be translated "All my life's why's and when's and where's and wherefore's are in God's hands."[3]

My times are in Thy hand;
Whatever they may be;
Pleasing or painful, dark or bright,
As best may seem to Thee.[4]

William F. Lloyd

10. In 31:16, what loving prayer did David offer to God? What does his request mean? (Please refer to Lesson Two, question 15 where a similar request was discussed.)

———————————————————

Have you ever prayed this request for your own life or the lives of others who are undergoing stormy events?

———————————————————

The psalmist was not only interested in having the ear of God (31:2), but also in placing his soul and life events in God's hand (31:5, 15). With all his heart he desired God's presence to be with him every hour of every day. The thought of God's lovely face shining on him as he endured uncountable stormy circumstances brought comfort and hope to his heart. It will do the same for us, for we need "no other sunshine than the sunshine of His face."[5]

Verses 17 and 18 contain additional requests for himself and prayers for wicked men with lying lips. Now the man after God's own heart (Acts 13:22) gives glory to God in 31:19–21 as he exalts His immeasurable goodness, protection, and kindness.

11. Verse 19 proclaims the goodness of Jehovah. Upon whom does God especially shower His goodness?

———————————————————

According to 31:20, how does God specifically care for His own when they are objects of strife and affliction?

———————————————————

12. What appropriate response to God's goodness did David express in 32:21?

———————————————————

How often do you praise Him for His marvelous goodness and kindness to you?

———————————————————

What are some good things God has provided in your life?

_____

_____

13. Have you ever questioned whether God is truly good *all the time*?

_____

What situations might cause believers, or unbelievers, to question His goodness? How would you answer these questions?

_____

_____

14. Our Good Shepherd speaks of His goodness throughout Scripture. How do the following verses declare His goodness?

Psalm 52:1

_____

Psalm 106:1

_____

Nahum 1:7

_____

James 1:17

_____

He Is Good—I Will Love Him More (Ps. 31:22–24)

15. After giving one more clear statement in 31:22 about answered prayer, David then wrote specific words for

"all [God's] saints." Read 31:23–24. What commands are found here?

_____

_____

Why would David feel it necessary to command "saints" to love their Lord? Should love for such a good God not be automatic? If saints do not love the Lord, then who will?

_____

_____

_____

What specific encouragements did the psalmist then give as reasons for loving the Lord?

_____

_____

It is the character of the saints that they do love God;
and yet they must be still called upon to love Him,
to love Him more, and love Him better, and show
proofs of their love.[6]

Selah—Pause and Think on These Things

- Psalm 31 is a holy song expressing many emotions. It is cherished because it is so human and yet truly divine. Especially to be loved are King David's names and descriptions of his God. To David, God was a rock and a fortress, a redeemer, and a God of truth. Gladly he testified of God's great and marvelous goodness and His power to hear and answer prayer. Before closing his great song, he wrote words of praise for the Lord who preserved him and had power to encourage and strengthen his very weak heart. We must never forget that all God was for David He is for us today. Oh, how great is His goodness!

- We need to take special notice of David's references to God's hands. Especially underline 31:5 and 15, for they paint a precious picture of David placing his life securely in the hollow of the Creator's mighty hands. When troubles come and we feel least able to hold on to God, it's not up to us. It's up to God to secure us, as He has promised, with His mighty hand.

I'll strengthen thee, help thee, and cause thee to stand,
Upheld by My gracious, omnipotent hand![7]

Robert Keen

- When was the last time you prayed, "Make thy face to shine upon thy servant"? David wrote Psalm 31 when he was alone and running from his enemies. How he hungered for God to be present with him in the long and dark days of his wilderness seclusion. Perhaps you are presently enduring long hard days with little hope of your life ever getting back to normal. Write out the words of 31:16, and make David's request your very own, along with the following words given long ago to all God's servants: "The Lord bless thee, and keep thee: the Lord make His face shine upon thee, and be gracious unto thee: the Lord lift up his countenance upon thee, and give thee peace" (Num. 6:24–26).

A Song of Instruction

I will instruct thee and teach thee in the way
which thou shalt go.
—*Psalm 32:8*

Scripture to read: Psalm 32:1–11

Although David was one of the greatest saints of
Scripture and one of the greatest sages of Scripture
and one of the greatest sovereigns of Scripture, he
was also one of the greatest sinners of Scripture.[1]

When confronted with his sins, a humbled, grieving David
repented and received forgiveness from the one he had sinned
against. This was followed by the writing of Psalm 51, in which
he promised he would teach transgressors God's ways (Ps. 51:13).
One way he accomplished this promise was through the writing
of Psalm 32, which he specifically called a *maskil* or psalm of instruction. For centuries God's people have been helped by reading the words of this royal instructor and then acknowledging
their own sin.

When the events of 2 Samuel 11 and 12 occurred, David
had served God for over thirty years. How could a godly man

commit such heinous sins? The same way all of us can if we choose to walk in our own ways. Let us read and prayerfully study this psalm, and let us receive its instruction carefully. Yes, David received complete cleansing when he cried to God, but his life and family were never the same. God will forgive our worst sins, but we must then live with the consequences. David's son Solomon testified to this the truth when he later wrote in Proverbs 13:15: "The way of transgressors is hard."

Psalm 32 can be divided into two sections: instruction from David in verses 1–7, and instruction from God in verses 8–11. There is a difference among good men regarding who is speaking in the last four verses.

Some say the entire psalm is David's words only (Joseph A. Alexander, Matthew Henry, and Peter Steveson). Others believe God spoke the healing words of verses 32:8–11 (John Phillips, W. Graham Scroggie, Charles H. Spurgeon). After weighing each opinion, I feel safe in standing with Phillips, Scroggie, and Spurgeon.

Instruction from a Pardoned Servant (Ps. 32:1–7)

As mentioned earlier, the details of David's spiritual collapse are recorded in 2 Samuel 11 and 12. Can you think of others in the Bible who not only had their sin exposed but also attempted to cover that sin? Also recorded for our learning are the words of Nathan, as he bravely confronted the king, and the sobering details of David's repentance and restoration.

1. Read 32:1–2. Both of these verses begin with the same word. What does the word *blessed* mean?

2. In these verses, a restored David shared four reasons his heart overflowed with happiness. What are these?

According to the psalmist, what had God done with his transgressions and sins?

3. David used four words to describe the awfulness of his sin: *transgressions*, *sin*, *iniquity*, and *guile*. Using a reliable Bible dictionary[2], define what each of these words means.

We would be astonished at the wickedness of David's sin if we did not know our own hearts!

4. When the prophet confronted the king about his sin, David fully repented (2 Sam. 12:13). Turn to Psalm 51:1–4, where his confession is also recorded. In these verses, what requests did a broken David make of his God?

Our merciful God heard David's cries, and 32:1 states God forgave him and covered his sins. What does it mean to have one's sins covered by Almighty God?

What a cover must that be which hides away forever from the sight of the all-seeing God all the filthiness of the flesh and of the spirit![3]

5. It is wonderful when God covers our sins as an act of mercy, remembering them no more (Heb. 8:12). Like David, many others have attempted to cover their sins

from our all-knowing God. What warning did Solomon give in Proverbs 28:13 regarding cover-ups?

_____

6. According to 32:3–5, David experienced a dark time in his life before he repented. Describe the turmoil experienced in his body and conscience as he attempted to conceal his wickedness.

_____

God will not allow any of His servants to get away with sin. Have you ever experienced God's heavy hand of conviction upon you?

_____

Why does God chastise, expose, and discipline His own? Read Hebrews 12:6 and Revelation 3:19.

_____

God is swifter to forgive than we are to confess.[4]

7. In 32:6–7, what comfort and security did the pardoned psalmist record for "every one that is godly"?

_____

What little word did David use to complete 32:4, 5, and 7?

_____

Though not exempt from all trouble, we are preserved, or kept from it. We are also surrounded continually by great songs, or psalms, of deliverance! Such amazing blessings call for us to pause because "love so amazing needs to be pondered, and joy so great demands quiet contemplation, since language fails to express it."[5]

Instruction from Our Pardoning God (Ps. 32:8–11)

The last four verses of Psalm 32 continue with helpful teaching. Our divine Instructor has given wonderful words of promise to those who have been pardoned. Within these final four verses, he has also included words of warning about stubborn individuals who sometime act like horses or donkeys!

8. Three comforting promises for God's children are found in 32:8. Write these below.

We have learned from David's earlier life the danger of walking in our own ways. What are the primary ways God uses to instruct and show us the paths where we are to walk? Read these verses for help with your answer:

Psalm 119:105

Psalm 119:130

2 Timothy 3:15–16

James 1:5

9. Read 32:9. What behavior might people sometimes copy from a horse or a mule?

Believers can indeed be like dumb animals! They can choose to be self-willed, stubborn, and rebellious. Such folks need to heed godly instruction on matters of restraint and submission because they are the opposite of the believers pictured in 32:8. Like David, they have often learned the hard way the blessing of being taught and guided by their merciful God.

10. The first clause of 32:10 is given as a warning to those who choose to walk in their own ways. What is the warning?

_____

The self-willed choices of such folks bring "many sorrows" into their lives. What sorrows might this include? See David's words in 32:3–4. Also read Proverbs 13:15 and Galatians 6:7–8.

_____

_____

11. A gracious promise concludes 32:10. What is the promise, and to whom is it given?

_____

_____

Throughout Scripture we read that our God is the Father of Mercies (2 Cor. 1:3) and that He is rich in tender mercies (Ps. 103:4). How would you define mercy?

_____

With what mercies has God surrounded you?

> Streams of mercy, never ceasing,
> call for songs of loudest praise![6]
>
> Robert Robinson

12. A pardoned David began this psalm with words of blessing. Our pardoning God concludes it with great

words of gladness and rejoicing. What important commands are given to believers in 32:11?

Selah—Pause and Think on These Things

- God did not allow even His choicest servant to escape the punishment of his sin. In exposing that sin, God included all the awfulness of David's adultery, murder, lying, and deceit. But we are also grateful that He records for us David's brokenness and repentance when confronted by Nathan. For our instruction, God directed his repentant servant to write Psalms 51 and 32. From these mighty songs we learn much about David's heart. Most of all, however, we are overwhelmed by the exceeding love and mercy of our pardoning God.

  In wonder lost, with trembling joy,
  We take the pardon of our God;
  Pardon for crimes of deepest dye,
  A pardon bought with Jesus' blood,
  A pardon bought with Jesus' blood.

  Who is a pardoning God like Thee?
  Or who has grace so rich and free?
  Or who has grace so rich and free?[7]

  Samuel Davies

- "The New Testament records nothing of David's sin. He is remembered by God, not for his moral failure, but as 'A man after mine (God's) own heart' (Acts 13:22)."[8] We are encouraged as we note that David is also honored in Hebrews 11:32 by having his name included with other great men and women of faith.

- We must never forget that there are definite consequences for sin (Gal. 6:7–8.)

Sin will always take us farther than we want to go, keep us there longer than we want to stay, and cost us more than we want to pay.

Author unknown

Promises, Promises!

*The eyes of the Lord are upon the righteous, and
his ears are open unto their cry.*
—Psalm 34:15

Scripture to read: Psalm 34:1–22

For many reasons, Psalm 34 has always been a favorite of mine. I have found myself returning to its words of comfort and promise regularly. Over the years I have come to think of it as a "land of promise" because of its multiple promises. David's great testimonies of answered prayer have also brought strength and hope to my heart on many occasions.

In this much-loved psalm, David wrote about God delivering him out of countless troubles. (The word *delivereth* is used four times in Psalm 34.) How we need to be set free from fear as well as our own troubles. We give special thanks for the angel of the Lord and his promised power to protect (34:7)! The angel of the Lord camped out wherever David resided, and the angel of the Lord is on duty for us, no matter where our paths may lead us.

Be sure to note the unique title given this psalm, for it is part of the inspired song. First Samuel 21 gives the unusual details that led to its writing, and these are not the most pleasant to read. David was hiding from King Saul who continually plotted to take his life. In desperation, David foolishly sought asylum among God's enemies, the Philistines—an unwise decision indeed since he had killed the great Philistine giant Goliath and was marked for death upon entering the land of God's enemies. Only by God's mercy was he delivered from this disobedience and collapse of faith.

There are no requests for God in this psalm, only testimonies of praise, along with treasured promises. We rejoice in David's boasting of God's faithfulness to him. We rejoice also as we read the promises and realize they are not given just for David. Yes, the promises truly are great! But we must not forget that they are so because of the greatness of the one who gave them to David.

David Boasting in God (Ps. 34:1–6)

1. According to 34:1, how often did David say he would praise his Lord?

   _____

   Someone has said that it is much easier to read this verse than to actually practice it. Why might it be hard to praise God at "all times" and "continually"?

   _____

   _____

2. What events in your life have sometimes made it difficult to praise God? Explain.

   _____

   _____

3. Read 34:2. In what other way did David seek to honor God?

   _____

People sometimes tire of hearing others boast. Why is bragging on God different? Why might "the humble" be glad to hear such boasting?

_____

_____

When was the last time you publicly "bragged" about the goodness and greatness of God?

_____

> We ought to talk of the Lord's goodness on purpose so that others may be confirmed in their trust in a faithful God.[1]

4. In 34:3, what two requests did the psalmist make of all who read his words?

_____

_____

In what ways might believers magnify (lift up) and exalt (praise) the Lord?

_____

Pure praise is the purpose of 34:1–3. Many years ago someone wrote that these words were David's "Hallelujah Chorus." He had much for which to give praise, and in 34:4–6 he shared some of those reasons.

5. Read 34:4 and 6. How did David express his urgent needs to God?

_____

How did God respond to this poor man as he cried for help?

_____

6. How amazing to realize that we, too, have the ear of the Almighty Creator day after day! What prayer testimony of God's faithfulness will you share today?

_____

_____

> We should continually keep in mind outstanding answers to prayer, and the deliverances God has wrought for us in the past. They should be like evergreens in memory's garden, so that we may be encouraged amid present difficulties to bless the Lord at all times.[2]

David Resting in God's Promises (Ps. 34:7–22)

All of God's Word is wonderful, but in this lesson we are especially giving thanks for the promises we find there. A promise is a sincere pledge to perform a specific thing. God did not have to promise anything to sinful men, but because of His love and mercy, He encouraged us by giving "exceeding great and precious promises" (2 Pet. 1:4). In Psalm 34, there are over a dozen promises given to the righteous. After we consider these, we will then look at 34: 16 and 21. Here we will see some of those sobering promises given to the wicked.

7. Read the following verses, and record what is promised to those who fear God. Please note that some verses contain two promises.

34:7

_____

34:8

_____

34:9

_____

34:10

34:15

34:17

34:18

34:19

34:22

8. Which of these promises are your favorites?

   With whom will you share one or more of these precious promises this week?

9. What promises are given to "those that do evil" and those "that hate the righteous"? The answer is found in 34:16 and 21.

> [God is] determinately resolved that the ungodly shall not prosper; He sets Himself with all His might to overthrow them. . . . Ungodly men only need rope enough and they will hang themselves; their own iniquities shall be their punishment. Oh

> happy are they who have fled to Jesus to find refuge
> from their former sins.[3]

Some may wonder if God, the Promiser, is able to remember and perform all He has promised. Friends, God cannot lie. "Hath He spoken and shall He not make it good?" (Num. 23:19). How we need to keep our eyes fixed upon the greatness of the Promiser, not just the promises themselves. We give thanks that with our God there are no breaches of promise! All He promised He is able to perform.

10. What do the following verses say about God fulfilling His promises?

1 Kings 8:56

_____

Nehemiah 9:8

_____

Romans 4:20–21

_____

> 'Tis so sweet to trust in Jesus,
> Just to take Him at His Word.
> Just to rest upon His promise,
> Just to know, "Thus saith the Lord."[4]

Louisa M. R. Stead

David Teaching the Fear of God (Ps. 34:11–14)

Before concluding our lesson, we need to return for a closer look at 34:11–14. The Bible declares that David was a faithful shepherd, a brave warrior, a skilled writer, a great king, and a beloved musician. We rarely think of him, however, as a teacher. And yet, in Psalm 34:11, King David issued an invitation to children, or sons, to hear him teach. This man after God's own heart desired to impart to others helpful truths that, if obeyed, would lead them to happiness.

11. According to 34:11, what specific truth did David wish to teach those who gathered around him?

_____

In 34:9, what similar truth had he commanded of all saints?

_____

The fear of the Lord is a foundational truth found throughout Scripture. It is seen often in the book of Psalms, as we have noted already in Psalms 19, 25, and 31.

12. What does it mean to "fear the Lord"? For help with your answer, consult Lesson Five.

_____

13. There is a universal desire to have a happy life that is filled with good things. How can we have such a life? Read 34:13–14 for help with your answer.

_____

Those who fear the Lord can have a good day every day. Why then, are many of our days anything but happy?

_____

> You can have a good day if you follow certain instructions from Scripture. Try following the guidelines of this psalm. Not only will you have a good day, but those with whom you come in contact will be blessed.[5]

Selah—Pause and Think on These Things

- David began Psalm 34 by making promises to his God. At all times, he promised there would be praise for God coming from his mouth. In 34:2, he also promised to boast about his loving and merciful Lord. As a believer, what promises have you made to God? How well are you fulfilling your promises?

- When was the last time you publicly "bragged" on God? "Let the redeemed of the Lord say so" (Ps. 107:2).

- A "promisee" is one to whom a promise is made. We who are promisees must be sure that we

  - know what God has promised us,
  - have faith in the Promiser and His promises,
  - keep the promises we make to God (Ps. 66:13–14),
  - share the promises to spiritually encourage others, and
  - regularly claim God's promises for ourselves and others.

- "Do not treat God's promises as if they were curiosities in a museum."[6] They are not simply words to be read and admired. No! They are to be claimed and shared as everyday sources of comfort and strength for ourselves and for those who may be fearful and ready to quit.

Trust His Word! Trust His Word!
All God's promises are true.
Trust His Word!
When your pathway disappears,
When your joy gives way to tears,
When you're plagued with doubts and fears,
Trust His Word![7]

Ron Hamilton

A Servant's Song

How excellent is thy lovingkindness, O God!
therefore the children of men put their trust
under the shadow of thy wings.
—Psalm 36:7

Scripture to read: Psalm 36:1–12

Before we read a word of Psalm 36 itself, we read its title and learn that David, the servant of the Lord, wrote it. We note also that it was written to the chief musician, or the temple choir director. This indicates it was to be sung in public worship.

David had many titles in life, but surely "the servant of the Lord" was the one that brought the most joy to his soul. It was not just a title he gave himself. No, it is the way God described this one so close to His heart (2 Sam. 7:5). We desire that the study of this short and remarkable psalm will draw each of us nearer to His heart and thereby result in additional profitable servants for our Lord.

Most of Psalm 36 paints a portrait of the graceless man (36:1–4) and a portrait of our gracious God (36:5–9). The servant ends his song with a brief prayer (36:10–12), asking God to continue His help and blessing in the lives of all who know Him. Will you ask

God to help you know Him in a greater way as you study this servant song?

The Servant Ponders (Ps. 36:1–4)

In the first nine lessons of this study, we have noticed how often David gives insight regarding evil and wicked servants of sin. Here, however, he reminds us for the first time "that wickedness begins with the rejection of God, and that the wicked person is characterized above all else by the fact that he does not take God into account."[1]

1. How do the first four verses describe the character and decline of the wicked?

   _____

   _____

   _____

   _____

2. According to 36:1, what is the greatest transgression of wicked men?

   _____

   According to 36:1, where does this great rebellion against God originate?

   _____

Sinful people refuse to recognize their sin and are not repulsed by it. Without God, they have nothing to restrain their wickedness. Above all else, they deny there is a God to whom they are accountable. Because they refuse to "retain God in their knowledge, God [gives] them over to a reprobate mind . . . being filled with all unrighteousness" (Rom. 1:28–29).

3. In 36:2–4, David stated that the wicked are unable to speak truth, to do good, or to be truly wise.

According to Proverbs 9:10, why is this so?

_____

4. It is a sobering truth that God will judge the wicked. What do the following verses state about this judgment?

John 12:48

_____

_____

Jude verses 14–15

_____

_____

Revelation 6:14–17

_____

_____

Revelation 20:11–15

_____

_____

> And, oh, what a weeping and wailing,
> As the lost were told of their fate;
> They cried for the rocks and the mountains,
> They prayed, but their prayer was too late.[2]
>
> B. H. Shadduck

The Servant Praises (Ps. 36:5–9)

We are glad that the psalmist abruptly turned from describing graceless creatures who acknowledge no evidence of God and never stand in awe of Him. Unlike the wicked ones who will not acknowledge God, a humble servant named David feared his Creator and continually praised His greatness. In 36:5–6, he asked us to join him in considering four comforting truths about our indescribable God. In 36:7–9, he then wrote about four blessings enjoyed only by the godly.

5. In 36:5, David speaks of two attributes of God— something that is true about Him. What are these?

_____

_____

Note: most translators define the word *mercy* as "unfailing love" or "loving-kindness."

6. How did David describe God's mercy?

_____

How true are these words of Charles Spurgeon: "When we can measure the heavens, then shall we be able to [measure] the mercy of the Lord."[3] In other words, it is immeasurable! Such is also the case with the attribute David mentioned next.

7. God's faithfulness is the second attribute found in 36:5. How would you define the faithfulness of God?

_____

In what ways has God shown His faithfulness to you and those you love?

_____

Simply stated, His faithfulness means He can be counted on to fulfill every word He has promised (Num. 23:19). Faithfulness denotes dependability, loyalty, and stability. Our hope rests on His faithfulness (Deut. 7:9). How wonderful to be a friend of the only one who is forever faithful!

8. Every day we are surrounded by His faithfulness. What should be our response to such faithfulness? For help with your answers, read the following verses:

Psalm 31:23

_____

Psalm 89:1–2

_____

1 Corinthians 4:2

_____

9. In 36:6, David wrote two additional magnificent truths about God. What are these?

_____

_____

10. Descriptions of His righteousness are found in Deuteronomy 32:4 and Psalm 145:17. After reading these words of Moses and David, write your own definition below.

_____

In 36:6, David likened God's righteousness to great mountains. What might this metaphor mean?

_____

God's judgment, or justice, concludes David's short list of attributes. We note that he was not writing of final judgment and punishment. Instead, he was referencing God's justice in human affairs. He is the righteous judge of all the earth, and all His judgments are fair, impartial, true, and right (Rev. 16:7). With the hymn writer Palmer Hartsough we can confidently say: "He is the true one, He is the just one, He hath the words of life!"[4]

11. What do the following verses reveal about God's justice?

Deuteronomy 10:17

Jeremiah 9:24

_____

1 John 1:9

_____

12. We are sinners, and God's just nature requires that
He punish all evil. If God gave us all we deserve, what
would happen to us? Find your answer in Romans 6:23.

_____

13. How did our loving, just God provide a way for us to
escape the punishment we deserve? Read 1 Peter 3:18
and Romans 3:21–24.

_____

According to Romans 5:1, what is the amazing result of
our justification?

_____

Having called our attention to four attributes of the Father,
the psalmist now writes in 36:7–9 of the fourfold blessings continually enjoyed by His children—blessings, by the way, that the
wicked refuse due to their self-deception and arrogance.

14. The first blessing for believers is found in 36:7. What
special dwelling place is always available to those who
enjoy His loving-kindness?

_____

David often hid himself in this "feathered" refuge. In the
following verses, what testimonies did he give about his
experiences in that safe abiding place?

Psalm 57:1

Psalm 61:4

Psalm 63:7

> Under His wings I am safely abiding,
> Though the night deepens and tempests are wild;
> Still I can trust Him, I know He will keep me,
> He has redeemed me and I am His child.
>
> Under His wings, O what precious enjoyment!
> There will I hide till life's trials are o'er;
> Sheltered, protected, no evil can harm me,
> Resting in Jesus I'm safe evermore.[5]
>
> William O. Cushing

15. The next two blessings of the righteous are found in 36:8. What do you think it means to be "abundantly satisfied with the fatness of [His] house"?

What does "drink of the river of [His] pleasure" mean?

Why are some believers not satisfied with all that God provides for them? Why do some never seem to hunger and thirst for the one who is the Water of Life? Perhaps some clues can be gleaned from Proverbs 3:5–7 and 4:23.

16. In 36:9, the psalmist proclaimed a great truth about life and light What is the source of this life and light ? See John 1:4, 9; 4:14; 14:6 for help with your answer.

_____

The words of 36:7–9 are "some of the most wonderful words in the Old Testament. Their fulness of meaning no commentary can ever exhaust."[6]

The Servant Prays (Ps. 36:10–12)

David concludes this delightful psalm with a brief prayer. He especially prays for others who know his God and are upright in heart. So far he has written of four attributes of God and four blessings enjoyed by His children. His brief prayer contains four specific requests, ending with a sobering prophetic glimpse of the wicked.

17. Read 36:10–11, and then list four requests David laid before God on behalf of the upright in heart.

_____

_____

_____

18. According to 36:12, what is the final doom of the workers of iniquity who according to 36:1 have "no fear of God before [their] eyes"?

_____

In the psalms we have studied so far, David has boldly prophesied the certain, sad ending of evildoers. Read the following verses from four of our earlier lessons and record what God says will be their certain end.

Psalm 1:6

_____

Psalm 8:2

Psalm 27:2

Psalm 34:21

Selah—Pause and Think on These Things

- In Psalm 36, we are given only four of God's attributes. Every believer must make it his life's goal to know what God is like. In His Word, God has described Himself in such a way that we are without excuse if we do not know His character. Charles Spurgeon said that the Bible's revelation of God is "what God declares Himself to be, what His people find Him to be, what all men will ultimately find Him to be."[7]

- "Poor, unsaved men have nothing but judgment ahead of them; but the children of the Lord have nothing but glory."[8]

- Let us make David's resolution our own: "In the shadow of thy wings will I rejoice" (Ps. 63:7). God has no wings, of course. The reference is to a mother hen with wings. How welcome are her chicks when sudden danger hovers near. This image may seem low when applied to Almighty God, yet it aids our understanding and helps us to remember this divine truth. The mighty wings of God provide a delightful and peaceful retreat in our times of trouble. As the hen loves to cover her little ones, so our God rejoices over us with joy, and we are forever safe and secure under the mighty shadow of His wings.

> Under His wings, what a refuge in sorrow!
> How the heart yearningly turns to His rest!
> Often when earth has no balm for my healing,
> There I find comfort, and there I am blest.[9]
>
> William O. Cushing

LESSON ELEVEN

GUIDELINES FOR GODLINESS

The law of his God is in his heart;
none of his steps shall slide.
—Psalm 37:31

Scripture to read: Psalm 37:1–40

In 1 Chronicles 29:28, God wrote a very brief obituary of His servant David. He recorded that David "died in a good old age, full of days, riches and honour." Many believe it was in his old age that the "sweet psalmist of Israel" (2 Sam. 23:1) wrote the majestic Psalm 37. They conclude this because of his testimony in 37:25: "I have been young, and now am old." In his testimony, he wrote of some things he had never observed (37:25), as well as things he had (37:35–36), in his long life of more than seventy years (2 Sam. 5:4–5).

After walking and communing with God all his days, David sat down to write this song of wisdom for others desiring to be men or women after God's own heart. This is the longest psalm we have considered in this study, and it is filled with needful guidelines for those seeking to be godly. It is another psalm that contains no prayer requests and no praise but lots of guidelines for godliness.

In Psalm 37, you will find additional references to a favored topic of the king—wicked and evil men. Because we have already considered this topic more than once, we will not dwell on it here. Instead, our focus will be on eight helpful guidelines that will keep us on the path to godliness. Whether you are young or you once were, careful obedience to these eight guidelines will help you be a woman who has a heart for God.

Guideline 1—No Fretting! (Ps. 37:1–2)

To fret means to get overheated or to get worked up. In the New Testament, the word *anxious* is usually used to describe such a person. Perhaps David mentioned fretting first because a person who is continually fretting will probably not obey the other guidelines that are to follow.

1. In 37:1, David commanded readers to calm down and avoid anxiety about and envy of whom?

    _____

    How might believers get "worked up" over evil men who enjoy flaunting their wickedness?

    _____

2. According to 37:2, why is our worrying unnecessary?

    _____

There is a cure for fretting, and it is faith in our sovereign God. A fretful heart is not a trusting heart. May we remember that having a little faith is not a little sin! These are words to remember as we consider the next guideline.

Guideline 2—Trusting God (Ps. 37:3)

Trust is the Old Testament word for faith. It means to believe in and have confidence in our God. It is a repeated truth throughout Scripture, especially in the psalms. David has touched on trusting God in at least three of the Psalms we have already studied.

3. What two commands did David give in 37:3?

To show we are trusting God, what "good" activities might we do for Him and others?

4. Two additional commands are given in 37:3 to those who trust and do good. What are these, and what do you think they mean? (For help with your answer you may want to check a Bible translation like the New King James Version, the New American Standard Version, or the English Standard Version.)

Guideline 3—Delighting in God (Ps. 37:4)

5. A wonderful command with promise is found in 37:4. What is the command?

It is not a burden to know God, and to walk with Him. No! Such a relationship is entirely delightful. What are some reasons many believers do not delight themselves in God?

6. In 37:4, what is promised to those who find their delight in Jehovah?

_____

One author has said this promise does not mean God will give us any foolish thing we may long for. It means that if we are delighting in God and longing for God, He will give us greater knowledge of Himself. God often rewards those who delight in Him with more than they can ever ask or think. What is your testimony of blessings that have been yours when you put God first and delighted in Him?

_____

_____

Guideline 4—Committing to God (Ps. 37:5)

7. Two definite commands are found in 37:5. First, we are to commit our ways to Him. This means we are to roll our load, or burden, on Him. Secondly, we are to trust Him. What concerns and burdens are you presently committing to Him?

_____

_____

Do you believe He is able to do as He has promised? What promises are you claiming as you wait on Him?

_____

_____

Write the encouraging promise found in 37:5.

_____

"What will He bring to pass? God will bring to pass the thing that does you the most good and that brings Him the most glory."[1] If God is going to accomplish anything for us, we must follow His instructions: commit all to Him and trust Him.

Guideline 5—Resting in God (Ps. 37:7–9)

8. Read 37:7–9. After committing our ways to God, David tells us at least six actions to take until God makes His will known to us. List these below.

_____

_____

Which of these do you find hardest to obey, and why do you think David listed two of these actions (waiting and not fretting) twice in these verses?

_____

_____

9. Someone has said it is often easier to react than to relax or rest. Do you agree? Explain.

_____

_____

What help and encouragements do the following verses offer to those who have trouble resting, waiting, and staying calm?

Psalm 46:10

_____

_____

Psalm 62:5, 8

_____

_____

Guideline 6—Following God (Ps. 37:23–24)

Two of the loveliest verses in Psalm 37 are verses 23 and 24. Here we find that all the events of a believer's life are "graciously ordained, and in lovingkindness [are] fixed, settled, and maintained. No reckless fate, no fickle chance rules us; our every step is the subject of divine decree."[2]

10. Does the godly woman always delight in the steps God ordains for her life? What steps, or paths, have been especially difficult for you to describe as delightful?

_____

_____

11. Painful paths may cause even the godly to fall into sin or into trouble. According to 37:24, how does our loving Father stand by to help His fallen children?

_____

How wonderful that we are helped back on our feet by His tender hand and that then His mighty hand continues to hold us up. This truth brings comfort to those who are after God's own heart, does it not? With His face shining on us (Ps. 31:16), His eyes watching all the events of our lives (Ps. 33:18), and His ears open to hear our cries (Ps. 34:15), why would we not want to give our hearts fully to follow Him?

> Through the love of God our Savior,
> All will be well;
> Free and changeless is His favor,
> All, all is well.
> Precious is the blood that healed us;
> Perfect is the grace that sealed us;
> Strong the hand stretched forth to shield us;
> All must be well.[3]
>
> Mary Peters

Guideline 7—Speaking for God (Ps. 37:30–31)

12. The words of our mouth always reveal our heart's contents (Matt. 15:18–19). In 37:30, how did David describe the speech of a righteous person? Does this describe your mouth?

_____

13. According to 37:31, where does a godly person learn of God's wisdom and judgments?

_____

The last part of this verse reveals the result of filling our hearts with His law. What is this?

_____

In 37:30–31, we are reminded that God is very concerned about our mouths, our hearts, and our feet. "When God's law is in your heart, He can do something through you and in you and for you. If the truth of God is in your heart, then the Word of God will be on your lips, and your feet will be walking on right paths."[4] May we seek to always glorify God with our mouths, our hearts, and our feet!

Guideline 8—Strengthening from God (Ps. 37:37–40)

As David concluded Psalm 37, he asked us once again to carefully contrast the upright man and the wicked man.

14. Read 37:37. Here we are told to observe the godly man. What is this man's future?

_____

According to 37:38, what is the future of those who delight to transgress against God?

_____

15. We are glad the psalmist ended his song by turning again to focus on the riches of all who are right with God. 37:39–40 speak of multiple blessings enjoyed by the righteous. What are they?

_____

_____

Why do the godly have access to such rich treasures? Your answer will be found in the last five words of this mighty psalm.

_____

> Trust Him when dark doubts assail thee,
> Trust Him when thy strength is small,
> Trust Him when to simply trust Him
> Seems the hardest thing of all.[5]
>
> Lucy A. Bennett

Selah—Pause and Think on These Things

- The reason many Christians do not trust in God, delight in God, entrust their way to Him, and rest in Him while waiting to know His will is that they do not know Him. The reason for this ignorance is simple: they do not spend time with Him. They do not know how truly great and gracious He is. Knowing God always involves daily personal fellowship with Him. What a wonderful, amazing God He is, for He stoops to ask for the fellowship of poor, sinful folks like us. Selah!

- We are grateful for David's divine words regarding the ordering of our steps by the Lord. I usually find it easier to agree with those words when my steps are found on happy and joyful paths, don't you? However, the test of our trust in Him is when we humbly acknowledge that paths leading to unemployment offices, chemotherapy treatments, doctor's offices, hospitals, and funeral homes have also been ordered by Him.

All things work out for good, we know,
Such is God's great design;
He orders all our steps below
For purposes divine.

Someday the path He chose for me
Will all be understood;
In heaven's clearer light I'll see
All things worked out for the good. [6]

John W. Peterson

Something to Sing About!

And he hath put a new song in my mouth,
even praise unto our God.
—Psalm 40:3

Scripture to Read: Psalm 40:1–17

The author who called Psalm 40 an exceedingly precious song was absolutely correct! Guided from above, Israel's great psalmist picked up his pen and wrote of patiently waiting on Jehovah. At the same time he urged God not to wait, but to hurry up with needed answers to his cries!

While reading Psalm 40, you may notice several familiar themes that have appeared in psalms we considered earlier. Waiting on God would be one such theme. Others include God's faithfulness, loving-kindness, and righteousness. Once again there are also references to David's multitude of enemies, his trust in God, crying out to God, and delighting in Him. These reoccurring themes make Psalm 40 the perfect "summation song" for these lessons.

In addition to repeated themes, five verses of this congregational song (40:13–17) are almost identically repeated in Psalm 70. The Holy Spirit surely knew our hearts needed the message of these words, so He directed that they be used more than once! May we take double heed to their message.

Psalm 40 is often called a "typically messianic"[1] song because of 40:6–8. Centuries before the incarnation of Jesus Christ, the Holy Spirit led David to describe a Greater David who would one day offer Himself once as the perfect sacrifice for our sin. The author of Hebrews also quoted David's words in Hebrews 10:5–7.

The psalm is easily divided into two sections. The first ten verses contain beautiful words of praise for past deliverance. Verses 11–17 then close with prayer for present dilemmas. Surely 40:17 is one of the most beautiful in all of the psalms. Here we find priceless words of comfort and help for all who are poor and needy. Such words certainly give us something to sing about!

Praise for Past Deliverance (Ps. 40:1–10)

1. In 40:1, how did David describe his attitude while waiting for the Lord?

   _____

   Author Elizabeth Elliot once wrote that waiting on God means to remain in readiness to *follow* orders, not to *give* them. A waiter does not give orders; he receives them. I want to wait on God this way—patiently, quietly, watchful, and attentive. Would you call yourself a patient waiter? Explain.

   _____

2. In 40:1–3, David wrote of several ways God rewarded his patience. Write these below.

   _____

   _____

3. In these same verses, we note several metaphors David used to describe his hopeless and desperate situation. What "slimy pit" are you in today? Perhaps it is a pit of sin or one of defeat and discouragement. Or it may also be a pit of deadly habits or other severe circumstances. What was the first step David took to get out of his slimy circumstances? Read 40:1 again.

_____

Are you following the psalmist's example as you seek deliverance?

_____

4. In God's time, the psalmist went from sinking to standing to singing! How did his testimony affect others who were observing his remarkable move from the mire to the choir? See 40:3 for your answer.

_____

5. David's testimony of his merciful rescue continued in 40:4. What paths to blessing, or happiness, are given here?

_____

6. The psalmist's testimony continues in the next verse. "His emotions took hold of David as he thought of God's goodness, and he uttered a marvelous statement of praise"[2] in 40:5. Using your own words, paraphrase David's inspiring praise to God.

_____

_____

_____

_____

_____

What are some of God's innumerable blessings in your life?

_____

_____

When our lives are full of mercy and blessings, they should also be full of gratefulness!

Almost all commentators believe that 40:6–8 speak specifically of our Lord Jesus Christ. Charles Spurgeon said of these verses, "Here we enter upon one of the most wonderful passages in the whole of the Old Testament, a passage in which the incarnate Son of God is seen."[3] The sacrifices and offerings mentioned here refer to religious rituals. The writer of Hebrews plainly states that no religious ritual can cleanse us of our sins (Heb. 10:11). Salvation is *by faith alone* in the finished work of our Savior who offered Himself as the *only* sacrifice for our sins (Heb. 10:12).

While 40:8 is part of the Messianic truth just mentioned, I would also like to apply its truth to all hearts who long to follow the Savior's example of doing the will of the Father.

7. What does it mean to do God's will?

_____

According to 40:8, what must be in our hearts if we are to know and do His will?

_____

8. David had an attitude of delight as he sought to do the will of God. What does this mean?

_____

The word *delight* was also used by David in Psalm 37:4. What promise did he give to all who delight themselves in the Lord?

_____

Would you, or other believers, describe your walk with God as "delightful"?

_____

When our hearts are delighting in His will, then we are close to His heart! May we always do His will "from the heart" (Eph. 6:6).

9. David has more words of devotion to God in 40:9–10. Here he tells of two things He *had* done as he lived for God and three things he *had not* done. Write them below.

_____

_____

_____

_____

How are you openly declaring His faithfulness and salvation to family, friends, and others?

_____

_____

Prayer for Present Deliverance (Ps. 40:11–17)

At this point in the psalm, David turned from praising to praying. His troubles were so many he could not count them. He moved from enjoying the blue sky of blessings to brooding under the black clouds of trouble. "How typical this is of life! Triumph and travail alternate. Joy and sorrow chase one another. Our life is made up of hills and valleys."[4]

10. 40:11 is especially touching as King David implored the King of Kings to deliver him from the loss of what spiritual treasures?

_____

11. In the first part of 40:12, he revealed why he could not do without God's mercy, loving-kindness, and truth. What was causing him to have heart failure?

12. The psalmist knew where to go when overwhelmed with such heavy burdens. What kinds of help did he seek from God in the following verses?

    40:13

    40:14

    40:15

13. In 40:16, what is David's counsel to all who seek God?

    What is to be their continual motto, or doxology?

14. There are countless blessings in our lives for which we should seek to always magnify, or exalt, the Lord. 40:1–3, 10 have already reminded us of His goodness. Before sending this psalm to the chief musician, David mentioned three more blessings in 40:17. What are they?

> God's thoughts of you are many. Let not yours be few in return.[5]

His final petition in this comforting song is an urgent request for God. What is the request, and have you ever prayed a similar one when burdened with your own troubles?

Selah—Pause and Think on These Things

- Do you remember when you were here?

  I was sinking deep in sin,
  far from the peaceful shore,
  Very deeply stained within,
  sinking to rise no more.[6]

  James Rowe

- Do you remember when the Master heard your cry, as He did David's (40:1)? We praise Him for helping us to *stand* on the Rock (40:2), for giving us a new song to *sing* (40:3), and new praises to *speak* (40:9–10). We must never forget the wonderful day we went from sinking to standing to singing and to speaking for our blessed Redeemer! This is certainly something to sing about!

  Hallelujah! what a Savior;
  Who can take a poor, lost sinner,
  Lift him from the miry clay and set him free!
  I will ever tell the story,
  Shouting, "Glory, glory, glory!"
  Hallelujah! Jesus ransomed me.[7]

  Julia H. Johnston

- Psalm 40:17 is a wonderful verse to end our study of selected psalms. King David stood in awe of the King of Kings as he penned the final words of Psalm 40. The humble king knew well that he was spiritually "poor and needy." That being his sad condition, why then would the King of all creation, the

Ruler of the universe, take time to think kindly of him? What condescension that He would think of any of us! And yet this He faithfully does all the days of our lives—something else, reader, for us to sing about!

- Over the years I have found the book of Psalms to be an irreplaceable gold mine of counsel and comfort. Woven into every one of these inspired songs are truths about our mighty God and His unfailing love for poor and needy folks like us. In this study, we have looked at only thirteen of these treasures, and what soul food we have seen displayed there! My prayer is that you will regularly—even daily—be found digging for gold in some of the 150 songs of our holy hymnal.

More to be desired are they than gold,
yea, than much fine gold. . . .
Moreover by them is thy servant warned:
and in keeping of them there is great reward.
—Psalm 19:10–11

Notes

LESSON ONE

1. William Jay, *Evening Exercises* (Harrisonburg, VA: Sprinkle Publications, 1999), 486–87.

2. Lloyd J. Ogilvie, *Falling Into Greatness* (Nashville, TN: Thomas Nelson Publishers), 18.

3. Charles H. Spurgeon, *The Treasury of David*, vol. 1, part 1 (McLean, VA: MacDonald Publishing Company, n.d.), 2.

4. Brian L. Webster and David R. Beach, *The Essential Bible Companion to the Psalms* (Grand Rapids, MI: Zondervan, 2010), 37.

5. Warren W. Wiersbe, *Wiersbe's Expository Outlines on the Old Testament* (Wheaton, IL: Victor Books, 1993), 430.

6. Frank M. Davis, "Out of Christ, Without a Savior" (1894).

7. Joseph Tyrpak, "O How Vast the Blessings" (churchworksmedia.com, 2008).

LESSON TWO

1. Spurgeon, 23.

2. Spurgeon, 34.

3. Elizabeth Clephane, "Beneath the Cross of Jesus" (1868).

4. Frances Havergal, "Take My Life and Let It Be" (1874).

LESSON THREE

1. *The Psalter*, "8. Lord, Our Lord" (1912).

2. Ibid.

3. Spurgeon, 81.

4. Webster and Beach, 44.

5. John Phillips, *Exploring Psalms* (Grand Rapids, MI: Kregel Publications, 2002), 1:68.

6. Spurgeon, 82.

7. Ron Hamilton, "How Majestic Is Thy Name" (Greenville, SC: Majesty Music, Inc., 1978).

LESSON FOUR

1. Warren Wiersbe, *Be Worshipful* (Colorado Springs, CO: David C. Cook, 2004), 81.

2. Author unknown, "Fairest Lord Jesus" (17th century).

3. Warren Wiersbe, *Be Worshipful*, 84.

4. *Scottish Psalter*, "Psalm 19" (1880).

LESSON FIVE

1. Peter A. Steveson, *Psalms* (Greenville, SC: Bob Jones University Press, 2007), 29.

2. Charles. H. Spurgeon, *The Golden Alphabet* (Pasadena, TX: Pilgrim Publications, 1969), 167.

3. Charles Edwards, *Treasury of Daily Devotions* (Greenville, SC: Ambassador Publications, 2003), devotion for May 4.

4. Charles Wesley, "Jesus, Lover of My Soul" (1740).

5. Thomas Kelly "When We Cannot See Our Way" (1815).

6. John Phillips, 1:189.

7. Katharina von Schlegel, "Be Still, My Soul" (translated 1855).

Lesson Six

1. F. B. Meyer, *Choice Notes on the Psalms* (Grand Rapids, MI: Kregel Publications, 1984), 39.

2. Peter A. Steveson, 110.

3. Joseph A. Alexander, *Commentary on Psalms* (Grand Rapids, MI: Kregel Publications, 1991), 129.

4. Leila Morris, "Nearer, Still Nearer" (1898).

5. John MacArthur, *The MacArthur Study Bible* (Nashville, TN: Thomas Nelson Bibles, 1997), 765.

6. Robert Robinson, "Come Thou Fount of Every Blessing" (1813).

7. Spurgeon, *Morning and Evening*, 381.

LESSON SEVEN

1. Spurgeon, *Morning and Evening*, 481.

2. Isaac Watts, "My Heart Rejoices in Thy Name" (1740).

3. W. Graham Scroggie, *A Guide To The Psalms* (Grand Rapids, MI: Kregel Publications, 1995), 184.

4. William F. Lloyd, "My Times are in Thy Hand" (1824).

5. Clephane.

6. Matthew Henry, *The Matthew Henry Commentary* (Grand Rapids, MI: Zondervan Publishing House, 1961), 608.

7. Robert Keen (?), "How Firm a Foundation" (c. 1787).

LESSON EIGHT

1. Phillips, 240.

2. The author finds these two dictionaries helpful as she reads Scripture: *Smith's Bible Dictionary* (Nashville, Thomas Nelson, 2004) and *Vine's Complete Expository Dictionary of Old and New Testament Words* (Nashville, Thomas Nelson, 1996).

3. Spurgeon, *The Treasury of David*, vol. 1, part 2, 81.

4. Scroggie, 187.

5. Spurgeon, *The Treasury of David*, vol. 1, part 2, 84.

6. Robert Robinson, "Come, Thou Fount of Every Blessing" (1758).

7. Samuel Davies, "Great God of Wonders" (1769).

8. Juanita Purcell, *Be Still My Child* (Schaumburg, IL: Regular Baptist Press, 1997), 138.

LESSON NINE

1. Spurgeon, *The Treasury of David*, vol. 1, part 2, 123.

2. J. Sidlow Baxter, *Awake My Heart* (Grand Rapids, MI: Zondervan Publishing House, 1960), 291.

3. Spurgeon, *The Treasury of David*, vol. 1, part 2, 126–27.

4. Louisa M. R. Stead, "'Tis So Sweet to Trust in Jesus" (1882).

5. Warren W. Wiersbe, *Prayer, Praise and Promises* (Grand Rapids, MI: Baker Books, 2011), 84.

6. Charles H. Spurgeon, *Spurgeon's Sermon Illustrations* (Grand Rapids, MI: Kregel Publications, 1990), 136.

7. Ron Hamilton, "Trust His Word" (Greenville, SC: Majesty Music, Inc., 1997).

LESSON TEN

1. James Montgomery Boice, *Psalms, Volume 1* (Grand Rapids, MI: Baker Books, 1994), 309.

2. B. H. Shadduck, "The Great Judgment Morning" (1894).

3. Spurgeon, *The Treasury of David*, vol. 1, part 2, 159.

4. Palmer Hartsough, "I Am Resolved" (n.d.).

5. William O. Cushing, "Under His Wings I Am Safely Abiding" (1896).

6. Spurgeon, *The Treasury of David*, vol. 1, part 2, 166.

7. Spurgeon, *The Treasury of David*, vol. 3, part 2. (McLean, VA: MacDonald Publishing Co, n.d.), 399.

8. H. A. Ironside, *Psalms* (Neptune, NJ: Loizeaux Brothers, 1952), 219.

9. Cushing.

LESSON ELEVEN

1. Wiersbe, *Prayer, Praise and Promises*, 94.

2. Spurgeon, *The Treasury of David*, vol. 1, part 2, 176.

3. Mary Peters, "Through the Love of God Our Savior" (1847).

4. Wiersbe, *Prayer, Praise and Promises*, 100.

5. Lucy A. Bennett, "Trust Him When Thy Wants are Many" (1876).

6. John W. Peterson, *All Things Work Out for Good* (Scottsdale, AZ: John W. Peterson Music, 1961).

LESSON TWELVE

1. Steveson, 158.

2. Steveson, 160.

3. Spurgeon, *The Treasury of David*, vol. 1, part 2, 237.

4. Scroggie, 234.

5. Spurgeon, *The Treasury of David*, vol. 1, part 2, 237.

6. James Rowe, "Love Lifted Me" (1912).

7. Julia H. Johnston, "There's a Sweet and Blessed Story" (1916).